W9-AEA-356

APACHE

Big Buddy Books
An Imprint of Abdo Publishing
www.abdopublishing.com

Sarah Tieck

www.abdopublishing.com

Published by Abdo Publishing, a division of ABDO, PO Box 398166, Minneapolis, Minnesota 55439.
Copyright © 2015 by Abdo Consulting Group, Inc. International copyrights reserved in all countries. No part
of this book may be reproduced in any form without written permission from the publisher. Big Buddy Books™
is a trademark and logo of Abdo Publishing.

Printed in the United States of America, North Mankato, Minnesota.
052014
092014

THIS BOOK CONTAINS
RECYCLED MATERIALS

Cover Photo: © Native American - Indian culture/Alamy.
Interior Photos: ASSOCIATED PRESS (pp. 13, 17, 30); Getty Images (pp. 9, 15, 29); © George H.H. Huey/Alamy
    (p. 19); iStockphoto (p. 26); © NativeStock.com/AngelWynn (pp. 5, 17, 23); Popperfoto/Getty Images (p. 25);
    © Anders Ryman/Alamy (pp. 16, 19); Shutterstock (pp. 11, 21, 23, 27).

Coordinating Series Editor: Rochelle Baltzer
Contributing Editors: Bridget O'Brien, Marcia Zappa
Graphic Design: Adam Craven

Library of Congress Cataloging-in-Publication Data

Tieck, Sarah, 1976-
 Apache / Sarah Tieck.
    pages cm. -- (Native Americans)
  ISBN 978-1-62403-351-3
 1. Apache Indians--History--Juvenile literature. 2. Apache Indians--Social life and customs--Juvenile literature. I.
Title.
  E99.A6T54 2014
  979.004'9725--dc23
                      2014005027

CONTENTS

Amazing People 4

Apache Territory 6

Home Life 8

What They Ate 10

Daily Life 12

Made by Hand 16

Spirit Life 18

Storytellers 20

Fighting for Land 22

Back in Time 26

A Strong Nation 28

Glossary 31

Websites 31

Index 32

Amazing People

Hundreds of years ago, North America was mostly wild, open land. Native Americans lived on the land. They had their own languages and **customs**.

The Apache (uh-PA-chee) are a Native American nation. They are known for their brave fighters and strong leaders. Let's learn more about these Native Americans.

Did You Know?

The name *Apache* means "enemy." It is believed that it came from the Zuni tribe.

Modern Apaches stay connected with the clothes and objects of their people's past.

Apache Territory

Apache homelands were mostly in the southwestern United States. This includes parts of present-day Arizona, Colorado, New Mexico, Texas, and northern Mexico. Land in the Southwest has mountains, deserts, canyons, and forests. It is rich in **minerals**.

The Apache nation was made up of many tribes that were spread out. The main tribes included the Mescalero, the San Carlos, the Jicarilla, and the White Mountain Apache.

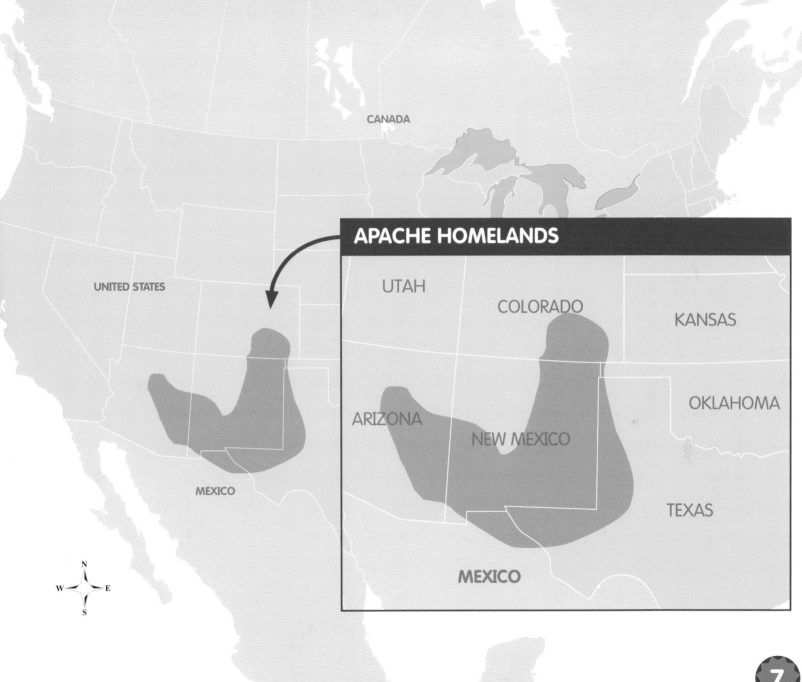

APACHE HOMELANDS

CANADA

UNITED STATES

MEXICO

UTAH

COLORADO

KANSAS

ARIZONA

NEW MEXICO

OKLAHOMA

TEXAS

MEXICO

HOME LIFE

Most Apache lived in wickiups. A wickiup had one room inside. The Apaches had little or no furniture. A wickiup was easy to put up, take down, and move to a new spot. This let the Apache move quickly and leave little to show they'd been there.

The women were responsible for building these homes. To make a wickiup, they cut down young trees. Then, they bent them into an upside-down "U" shape. This made a frame. They covered it with long grass.

The entrance to a wickiup was often low. People bent down to enter. Inside, the ceiling was tall enough for them to stand.

What They Ate

The Apache were hunters and gatherers. They hunted foxes, deer, elk, turkeys, and buffalo. They gathered wild plants, such as mescal, from the land. Some Apache farmed corn, or maize. Many moved around from place to place in search of food.

Hunting deer and elk took skill and time. The Apache used the meat for food and the skin for clothes.

DAILY LIFE

The Apache lived in camps. Within a camp, people had different jobs. Men were warriors, hunters, or **medicine men**. Women cooked and did chores. They built the family homes and made clothes.

Children helped with chores. They played games that kept them active and in good shape. They also had dolls and toys.

Did You Know?

Some Apache children carried their dolls in small cradleboards.

Apache mothers carried their babies in cradleboards.

13

The Apache were strong fighters. They wanted to **protect** their land and way of life. They often attacked nearby settlers, other tribes, and US soldiers. They would take food or other things they needed.

Men were the main fighters. But if their camp was attacked, women would also fight to protect it.

Did You Know?

Some Apache children began learning to ride horses at age five! As adults, they would fight and hunt on horseback.

Apache men and growing boys spent many hours practicing hunting and fighting skills.

15

MADE BY HAND

The Apache made arts and crafts. These were forms of art, but they had important uses.

Decorated Clothing

Both men and women wore buckskin shirts, leggings, and moccasins. They decorated these with beads and fringe.

Beadwork

The Apache sewed shells, glass, and turquoise beads into clothing and shoes. They also made beaded jewelry.

Woven Baskets

The Apache wove baskets. This old art form was passed down through the tribes.

Bows and Arrows

Making weapons was also an art form. To make arrows, Apaches shaped rocks or metal to be pointed and sharp. They made bows from wood and animal parts called tendons.

Spirit Life

Religion was important to the Apache. They believed in a god and a **sacred** power they called *diye*. They believed all plants, animals, and humans had this power. They prayed, sang, and danced to bring more diye into their lives.

Medicine men led the people in special dances and **ceremonies**. The Apache honored life events such as birth, childhood, and old age.

Did You Know?

Children went through a special hair-cutting ceremony. This was done to bring good health as they grew up.

 One ceremony honored a child's first pair of moccasins. The child walked to the east in new clothes and shoes. This was to make sure he or she had a good life journey.

 Adult Apaches let their hair grow long. They believed it was bad luck to cut it.

STORYTELLERS

The Apache told stories to share history or lessons. Rules and laws were not written down. So, storytelling was also a way to teach each other rules. And, some stories were just for fun. Stories were often told at the beginning of **ceremonies**.

Did You Know?

Coyote and Big Owl appear in many popular Apache stories. These characters helped teach and entertain people.

One Apache story tells how
the creator made the Earth.

FIGHTING FOR LAND

Land was important to the Apache. In the mid-1800s, American settlers began to move west through Apache land. The Apache tried to live in peace with them. But soon, they fought over land.

In 1862, the US government set up Fort Bowie in Apache Pass. This helped **protect** settlers and soldiers. Still, Apache leaders fought for their people's land and rights. They included Cochise, Mangas Coloradas, and Geronimo.

Did You Know?

Mangas Coloradas was a powerful Apache leader. He was from the Chiricahua tribe. He led fights against Mexican settlers on Apache land.

Cochise was a famous Chiricahua Apache leader. He wanted his people to be safe. He died in 1874. Today, a statue honors him.

Today, Fort Bowie is a national historic site.

In the 1870s, after years of fighting, the US government told the Apache people to live on a **reservation**. Some Apaches said they would not live there and kept fighting. A famous Apache warrior named Geronimo led their fight. He surrendered to the US government in 1886.

 Geronimo was a Chiricahua Apache warrior. He wanted to protect Apache land. So, he fought against American settlers and soldiers during the 1870s and 1880s. He died in 1909.

BACK IN TIME

1749

On August 16, Spaniards and Apaches signed a peace treaty. It lasted more than 15 years.

1540

Spanish gold seekers first met the Apache.

1886

Geronimo and his warriors surrendered at Skeleton Canyon.

1964

Fort Bowie became a national historic site. It was set up by the US government to fight against Apache attacks in 1862. It was in Apache Pass.

1906

Geronimo's Story of His Life was printed. The warrior told his story to author Stephen M. Barrett.

2010

The US government counted about 63,000 Apache living in the country.

A Strong Nation

The Apache people have a long, rich history. They are remembered for their handmade baskets and U-shaped wickiups. They are also known for their long fight to **protect** their way of life.

Apache roots run deep. Today, the people have kept alive those special things that make them Apache. Even though times have changed, many people carry the **traditions**, stories, and memories of the past into the present.

Modern Apache honor their homelands and traditions.

"We are all the children of one God. The sun, the darkness, the winds, are all listening to what we have to say."

— Geronimo

GLOSSARY

ceremony a formal event on a special occasion.

custom a practice that has been around a long time and is common to a group or a place.

medicine man a Native American healer and spiritual leader.

mineral a natural substance that makes up rocks and other parts of nature.

protect (pruh-TEHKT) to guard against harm or danger.

reservation (reh-zuhr-VAY-shuhn) a piece of land set aside by the government for Native Americans to live on.

sacred (SAY-kruhd) connected with worship of a god.

tradition (truh-DIH-shuhn) a belief, a custom, or a story handed down from older people to younger people.

treaty an agreement made between two or more groups.

WEBSITES

To learn more about Native Americans, visit **booklinks.abdopublishing.com**. These links are routinely monitored and updated to provide the most current information available.

INDEX

Apache Pass **22, 27**

arts and crafts **16, 17, 28**

Barrett, Stephen M. **27**

Chiricahua Apache **23, 25**

clothing **5, 11, 12, 16, 17, 19**

Cochise **22, 23**

farming **10**

fighting **4, 12, 14, 15, 22, 24, 25, 27, 28**

food **10, 11, 14**

Fort Bowie **22, 23, 27**

Geronimo **22, 24, 25, 26, 27, 30**

homelands **6, 22, 25, 29**

hunting **10, 11, 12, 14, 15**

Jicarilla Apache **6**

language **4**

Mangas Coloradas **22**

Mescalero Apache **6**

Mexico **6, 22**

religion **12, 18, 19, 21**

reservations **24**

San Carlos Apache **6**

Skeleton Canyon **26**

Spain **26**

stories **20, 21, 28**

United States **6, 14, 22, 24, 25, 27**

White Mountain Apache **6**

wickiups **8, 9, 12, 28**

Zuni **4**